"What Barb Klein invites you into, 111 times, is nothing less than total heart intimacy – but not with her – *with yourself*. Her vulnerable ecstatic truth-telling is such potent companionship for this twisty-turvy life. Open to any page and befriend yourself, and you will be so grateful you did."

> ~Jennifer Louden, best-selling author of
> *The Woman's Comfort Book* and *The Life Organizer*

"*111 Invitations* is like a cup of warm herbal tea and a sunny morning on the porch: A nurturing blend of poetry, words, and questions that help us to pause, slow down and listen to the subtle wisdom that lies beneath our to-do lists and full days. Pull up a chair, get settled, and let Barb's writings soothe the busyness and shed the burdens so you can invite peace, calm, and blessings back into your heart."

> ~ HeatherAsh Amara, author of
> *Warrior Goddess Training*

"Barb Klein's *111 Invitations* moved me deeply, connected me to humanity and helped me remember we're all in this together. This beautiful, soulful collection of poems and prayers reminds us of the power of sitting with life's big questions and that often this act – in and of itself – is more important than arriving at the answers. I look forward to keeping this collection next to my bed as a touchstone and reminder that I can open, trust and let go, and everything will be more than all right."

> ~ Renee Peterson Trudeau, author of
> *The Mother's Guide to Self-Renewal: How to*
> *Reclaim, Rejuvenate and Re-Balance Your Life*,
> and *Nurturing the Soul of Your Family*

"Dig into these invitations the way you'd put your hand into a mystery sack of treats, pulling out carefully and with anticipation a delicious delight that will please your palette and your senses. With each treat will also be the bonus of discovering yourself within. Read and soar."

> ~Laura Berman Fortgang, author of
> *The Little Book on Meaning*

111
Invitations

Step into the Full Richness of Life

Embrace this life!
With love
Barb

Barb Klein

BALBOA
PRESS
A DIVISION OF HAY HOUSE

Cover Art Credit: Heaven McArthur
www.heavenmcarthur.com

Author Photo Credit: Paige Photography
www.paigephotony.com

Balboa Press books may be ordered through booksellers or by contacting:

Balboa Press
A Division of Hay House
1663 Liberty Drive
Bloomington, IN 47403
www.balboapress.com
1 (877) 407-4847

Because of the dynamic nature of the Internet, any web addresses or links contained in this book may have changed since publication and may no longer be valid. The views expressed in this work are solely those of the author and do not necessarily reflect the views of the publisher, and the publisher hereby disclaims any responsibility for them.

The author of this book does not dispense medical advice or prescribe the use of any technique as a form of treatment for physical, emotional, or medical problems without the advice of a physician, either directly or indirectly. The intent of the author is only to offer information of a general nature to help you in your quest for emotional and spiritual well-being. In the event you use any of the information in this book for yourself, which is your constitutional right, the author and the publisher assume no responsibility for your actions.

Any people depicted in stock imagery provided by Thinkstock are models, and such images are being used for illustrative purposes only.
Certain stock imagery © Thinkstock.

Print information available on the last page.

ISBN: 978-1-5043-5526-1 (sc)
ISBN: 978-1-5043-5528-5 (hc)
ISBN: 978-1-5043-5527-8 (e)

Library of Congress Control Number: 2016907278

Balboa Press rev. date: 07/27/2016

Dedication

I dedicate this book to my husband, Tom, my soul mate, partner, friend, rock, and biggest supporter. Thank you for always believing in me and grounding me, while helping me shoot for the stars.

Table of Contents

Foreword

It's been said that well-written words will move our hearts, wake us up and encourage us to settle into new patterns and new ways of being. After reading *111 Invitations,* from cover to cover, I felt as though my heart had been gently awakened and that my own journey to healing was somehow more understood.

Barb Klein is on a journey to awaken her soul. Each day she chooses to allow and surrender to what is, knowing that her own healing and growth sits just on the other side of each emotion or challenge that shows up. Barb has learned that it is the embracing of these situations that allows her to live her life fully. And live fully she does. Barb is committed to walking her talk and sharing her story and lessons with others around her who can be inspired and motivated by her lessons.

The emotions that arose within me as I read each chapter of this powerfully written book took me on a roller coaster ride back through the days when I was supporting my son through a serious health crisis. I was reminded of the moments of anger and feelings of abandonment as I was left to figure out how to find care, support, and treatment for an illness that I knew little about. As I read, I felt not only connected to the words but to Barb's heart and soul. Our stories are different and yet, the feelings and challenges resonated just the same.

Each section of this beautifully written book carried me along through the highs and lows of my son's illness and the starts and stops of my own story as I vacillated between despair and hope and despair again. I especially resonated with the invitations of acceptance and surrender and the reflection that followed this chapter. With each verse, Barb leads the reader through a deeper level of thought and understanding while never sugarcoating how easily one can be swallowed up by grief and challenges. And yet, if we are open to the possibilities, new perceptions and insights are often readily revealed.

This book opens possibilities for seeking and learning, healing and forgiving and overcoming even when it doesn't seem possible. It is an invitation to find our own version of peace in the midst of whatever life sends our way.

~ *Amy White*
Intuitive, Life Coach, and Caregiver Champion
International Best-selling Author, *Bold is Beautiful: Breakthroughs to Business Strategies*
San Francisco, CA

Opening

In July 2015, I entered a labyrinth in Taos, New Mexico on the eve of a much-anticipated writers' retreat. I entered with a spotted pink stone and a simple question: *How can I be true to myself this week?* Turmoil was brewing back home, and I could have easily been pulled out of myself and into worry.

As I walked, guidance came and I quickly found my own rhythm without hurrying to get to the center. It was about the journey – each step, *the next step*. That's all that mattered in the moment. I heard a voice from within ask me, *Can you really BE with yourself, right here, right now?* I settled in and overcame the urge to rush to the finish and the frustration at being turned away from where I was headed. The rushing and frustration felt very familiar – I often approach life this way. In that moment I became aware of how very unhelpful that is.

Arriving in the center of the labyrinth, I placed my stone on the altar with deep gratitude for the insight I had already received, and I began my winding departure back to where I had begun. I ventured to look up and out, inviting and welcoming new beginnings, knowing I would be led. I trusted my feet to fall on the path, and knew that if I bumped up against a rock, it was no big deal. I'd get back on the path. My eyes and heart opened as I slowed down, lifted my gaze, and breathed in the space around me – the majestic mountain vistas, the gently swaying trees, the exquisite New Mexico sky, the birds' beautiful flight and song. I soaked it all in with wonder, appreciation, and awe while moving forward in my own rhythm. Not stopping, getting stuck, or rushing, but simply noticing and savoring.

*   *   *

So it is in this labyrinth of life – twists, turns, uneven paths, shocks, joys, highs and lows all winding together in a journey that is unique to each of us. When I am able to remember that the richness of life truly does lie in the steps along the way and that there is no end goal to achieve, a sense of surrender, acceptance, and hope settles in. In those moments I flow with a little more grace and a little more ease. Yet, any life worth living carries moments of confusion, loss, grief, frustration, and anger. When I find myself resisting certain moments, wishing them away, a sense of dis-ease settles in.

For the past several years, I have walked a path where on one side land mines explode, one after the other, sometimes in rapid succession, destroying my world as I knew it to be. On the other side, hope, dreams, and passion flourish in a journey of deep connection with myself, discovering what lights me up, and claiming my purpose, passion, and power in this world.

It seems impossible to coexist in a space of such extreme contrasts. At times I have found myself whirling in the midst of these contradictions, not knowing where or how to find my ground. On the one hand, I have soared to new heights, buoyed by my courage to risk and to live my life fully and by a sea of support that never fails to amaze me. On the other hand, I've been stripped bare, cowering, torn and battered, looking at the shreds of life that lay around me. The gift has been in finding a way to center within the path, to step forward, inch by inch, into a new tomorrow or just into the next minutes. Somehow I've been pulled by an undying faith that I would endure and come out the other side, hopefully better and stronger than before.

The extreme powerlessness I experienced helped me to learn the lesson of letting go, while still loving. The pain of someone I deeply love does not have to be my pain. When it's my child who is suffering, I've learned that going down with him only leaves us both drowning, which serves no one. Days strike when I definitely sink, for sure, yet I know I can resurface and find my way in the world when I am ready.

The past few years have been a time of extremes and learning that the more I open my heart to love, joy, possibility, and hope, the greater is my risk for loss, sadness, heartache, and despair. I've felt it all. It's hard to express, and a lot to embody within one heart, one life, one soul. I've done the best I can to do just that.

There have been dark times when my son has been lost and unavailable to me as he's faced his own challenges. It's been extremely painful because I love so deeply, care so deeply, and am so strongly bonded to this child of mine. I have always held him close in my heart through a love even *I* don't understand. At times I've been able to step in and help; other times, all I could do was let go and pray for the best. Fear, uncertainty, and experiences I've never dreamt I would face haunted me. Anger, sadness, loss, grief, and deep, deep pain live too close to my heart. Self-doubt and self-flagellation find a home within me at times. In some ways, the scariest moments are those in which I dare to hope. Endless uncertainty still remains, as no one knows how this story will end. I'm learning that life is endless uncertainty. To think otherwise is to kid ourselves.

The very circumstances that have been so heart-breaking and challenging are also the ones that have awakened and opened my heart. These were the times that strengthened my relationships with myself, with my family, friends, and community. I learned lessons and accessed a deeper compassion, love, and purpose that would not have been possible had my life gone in a different direction. This journey has awakened my soul and called it forth to its true expression.

Strength, courage, and clarity have emerged in my life. Long periods of tension, worry, stress, and jaw clenching have driven me toward the counterbalance of extreme self-care and learning how to truly nurture, nourish, and honor myself. I've needed more rest and reflection, more pause and quiet, more stillness and gentleness. I've done what I've needed to in order to rise again and continue forward in the quest for the life I desire. I left a job that was no longer right for me to start my own business, doing work I love. I am absolutely passionate about helping people come home to themselves and claim their place in the world, beyond the roles that typically define them. I care deeply about helping others to discover how to honor and care for themselves, even in times of extreme stress. My hard times, challenges, and experiences of rising above have informed me, guided me, and led me to work that fulfills me and serves others. Overall, life is really good.

Joy, laughter, fun, peace, and celebration dance through my life, even when it seems impossible. I followed my heart's desire and travelled across the world to Australia to set sail on a writers' workshop in the South Pacific, officially launching my entry into the writing world. My relationship with my husband, Tom, has grown increasingly stronger as we've come together in partnership and love. We recommitted to one another after 24 years of marriage in a ceremony and celebration with 80 loved ones. It was one of the happiest days of my life, even though it required me to set aside simultaneous sadness and fear. We've enjoyed special family times, and moments of precious connection with those we hold dear.

To some extent I've had to learn the art of compartmentalization – being with the one piece of my life I'm in right now while setting others aside until a later time. Maybe that sounds unhealthy, but it's been a vital survival skill and one that has allowed me to do more than just survive.

No single story defines my entire existence – each story line is part of my whole truth and reality. No *one* story holds more weight than any other, unless I allow it to. The many stories of my life take turns driving me, lifting me up, and weighing me down. I am able to be present to my work and the people in my world – even at times when curling up in a fetal position and withdrawing from life is, oh, so tempting.

Through my work, I share what I learned in these tumultuous years. I coach, teach, write, and lead retreats to reassure people that the entire spectrum of life happens to all of us. We can feel what we feel and stay there for as long as we want, but we are always at choice. We direct our energy. We choose the meaning we attach to what's happening. Nothing will stay the same. This is a universal truth. We can keep ourselves stuck, or we can write a new story. We all have pain, sadness, loss, grief, powerlessness, confusion, and shame; this is part of our shared humanity. With this knowledge, we remember we are not alone, even when things feel very personal.

In *111 Invitations* you will see moments of despair and moments of great joy. Sometimes I am standing in the middle of both, and sometimes I am all in one or the other. Life is full and rich because of its contrast and contradiction. I am only now learning to embrace all of life in its entirety; to do so allows me to live life fully and wholeheartedly.

I suppose if my world hadn't crumbled so badly, I would not have been propelled to find another way. Some days I find myself reeling between the unimaginable pain of what my son has gone through and the unimaginable gifts and grace of support being given to me. I've decided not to try to make sense of it, but to just be with it. This is my journey.

While my journey is often topsy-turvy, I welcome this life over a safe, grey, neutral zone where nothing extreme happens. Sleepwalking through my days is not what I want – I am wide-awake and I am feeling it all. Sometimes I'm amazed that I get up and keep on going. But, taking life one day at a time, one moment at a time, has allowed me to continue on and even to soar at times. Sometimes I still lie in numb disbelief.

I'm not an extraordinary person. I am just another person who is finding her way through this labyrinth of life. I am living a life that has its own story lines, no better or worse than anyone else's – they're just mine. You have yours.

I have resisted writing my personal story, because I truly believe the personal details don't matter. At the same time I realize giving you some context for my writing is important. A purpose of sharing this book is to unmask our commonality. My story is my story and yet it is the universal story: joys, hopes, dreams and victories, pain, sadness, defeats, and loss. My entry to pain may or may not be the same as yours, but whether it comes through relationships, career, finances, addiction, illness, or death, we each know it and live it. I know you've overcome things other people can't even imagine. I know you have had dreams and found joy others will never know. We are in this life together – our lives may look different on the surface, but deep down, the underlying themes are the same.

Introduction

This book is a gift of invitations into the contrasts of life, to the wholeness of life, reminding you there is no joy without sadness, no light without dark, no beginning without ending, and no love without loss. Each invitation calls you to look at your own life. As you begin this book, ask yourself: *Am I willing to observe my life with eyes of wonder? Am I willing to question to find my own truth? Am I willing to be present with what life gives me as I delicately find my way to hold each moment's truths, gifts, lessons, and feelings? Can I simply be with myself when it's not simple at all? Can I allow the harshness of noise and disruption to simply land and touch upon my ears without defining me?* Life is an invitation, and these are some of its questions.

I trust you are holding *111 Invitations* because there is something here that will speak to your soul. My invitations to you, dear reader, may reveal your own life story and help you see its uniqueness and magnificence

As you read this book, you will find some pieces reflect very opposite emotions or experiences. Things can change quickly – particularly in our internal world – some of the pieces you will read were written within only hours of one another. Oftentimes "simply" changing our mindset reveals a fresh perspective that was elusive, invisible, or inconceivable not long before. Life is a never-ending dance and sometimes we flow beautifully with it, while other times its rhythm and steps feel out of sync or even disruptive to our core.

This book is structured in sections which reflect this twisty journey to capture the times when we feel as if we are moving forward easily and those times when we feel lost, confused, or as if we have gone astray.

I invite you to journey with me, knowing you are truly never alone. We are in this together, sharing life and its fullness – our stories unique, but our humanity shared. We are souls living a human experience, learning lessons along the way, at times lost and floundering, at other times flowing gracefully, and a lot of the time walking the straight and narrow path of the daily mundane. Beauty and gifts are everywhere, in the most joyous celebrations and even in the unrelenting dark. *Join me.*

I offer a collection of reflections on life's moments, feelings, and happenings. I offer a few prayers sprinkled throughout to tap the greater universal energy surrounding us. Read a particular section that calls you or open randomly and see where that page takes you. Each section offers space for your reflection as you integrate the reading into your own life.

I invite you to dog-ear pages, make notes in the margins, underline, star, highlight, and let your heart find what speaks to it today. Leave the rest. Find your own resonance where you will and make it your own.

My wish for you is to lovingly and gently greet and welcome yourself, exactly as you are, where you are moment to moment. I wish for you to release the need to fix or figure out that which is not yours. I wish for you to let go of any belief that there is anything within you that needs to be fixed. I wish you regular time to sit quietly with your questions and listen to your inner wisdom, just waiting to be tapped. I wish for you to take life as it comes, allowing yourself the grace to be where you are, and knowing whatever is up for you right now surely won't last.

My wish for you as you read *111 Invitations* is that you enter these pages with openness, curiosity, and a desire to know yourself a bit more deeply as you reflect on life through the wisdom of your heart. I invite you to look for places where you can stretch into territory that is a little uncomfortable or unfamiliar. My greatest wish is that you embrace and step boldly into the full richness of life with all of its uncertainty, in all its glory and all its pain.

Beginning

....

The First Invitation

Being born is life's first big invitation.
The angels smile lovingly upon you
with a whisper:
"Come, sweet little one.
Come grace the world with your gifts.
You are a light.
Come.
Shine brightly the glory that is you.
Come.
Learn your lessons.
Brighten the world.
Welcome.
We are so glad you are here.
Flow in grace
and be who you were born to be –
there is no other like you.
Come."

From your very first stirrings,
your very first breath,
life invites you to show up
and be all you were born to be.

Life calls you
to question, wonder, and discover
the world that awaits you.

I Sit on the Sidelines

I sit on the sidelines
enjoying the view –
nothing to risk here,
nothing at all.

Just be an observer…
put my head down,
avert my eyes.
No one will notice.
I like it that way.

I'll never be chosen
to enter the game.
I have nothing to offer –
no remarkable talents at all.

I'm content in this land
of nothing to lose.
It's safe and it's cozy.
I don't have to choose.

Sunrise to sunset.
The daily mundane –
mealtimes and bedtimes
mark my days.

How Often?

How often have I entered a space
trying to be invisible,
believing that no one
wants to know me,
hear me, or see me?
Believing it wasn't safe?

Denying even the attraction
from those who dare to approach
despite my fortress walls.

How often have I missed opportunities
for true connection
because I was too afraid
to let me out?

How often?

How much have I missed out on,
hiding in the wings,
shrouded in the dark,
daring not to be seen?

How many opportunities lost?
Friendships missed?

I look back to say good-bye,
not with regret for what might have been
but ready to step into what's possible.

I am grateful to have been protected,
while now I am ready for more!

A Prayer for New Beginnings

It is the dawn of a new day,
as each day is.
What lies before me is magical,
unknown, unseen…
My heart is open, and I feel the pull.
To what? I wonder.

I soak in the beautiful energy of
stirring within.
I'm coming alive.
The time is now.
It's always NOW.
Why not? Why wait? I hear myself say.

What if?
Magnificent possibilities await.
Just take a step
and listen…
Listen for the small voice within.
It beckons.
It vibrates.
My heart knows the answer.
All I need to do is listen, hear,
show up, open and ready.

Reflection on Beginning

For much of my life, I fought a battle within myself – a running story telling me it wasn't safe to be seen and heard, yet I somehow mysteriously found myself repeatedly stepping into roles of leadership. I was compelled to show up in a way that wasn't fully comfortable. And, I was fighting who I truly was – unwilling or frightened to claim my space and to claim myself. I didn't know what to do with the ways life was calling to me, inviting me to show up. I didn't totally believe I mattered.

Take a moment now to reflect on your own life with love, acceptance, reverence, and appreciation for where you've been and who you've become because of the unique path you have journeyed. Who were you then and who are you now?

We are always in a state of transition, so we are always at some stage of beginning. At times it's hard to see clearly where we are heading or even where we are right now. Take a few moments to think about where you are and imagine where you might be heading.

Begin Anew

....

Wake Up!

Conscious living,
mindful choices,
being awake and aware...
herein lies the magic
to creating the life
I desire
and deserve.

Too often we float through life
in a dream-like trance,
sleep walking through the motions,
unaware of what we're doing,
paying no attention,
losing time in moments
and days.

Wake up!
Wake up and choose
who I want to be,
how I want to be,
and what this beautiful life of mine
will look like today.

What will it reflect about me?
How will it nourish me?
What will be meaningful,
fulfilling, and exciting,
in a life lived consciously?

How will I spend my time?
Who will be with me?
How will I honor my body and spirit
this day?

Yes!

A world of possibilities
lies in wait,
ready to be discovered,
ready to be explored.

Open the door,
throw back the gates,
step in,
look around.

It's wondrous
and exciting!
Scary and new.

The choices are yours,
and the power is too.

Where will you go
on this magical ride?

Are you open to see,
without knowing?

Where will life take you
when you show up
and say "yes!"?

Throw open your arms,
declare yourself ready, and
witness the wonders that unfold.

Look through the Eyes of Love

Do you see the goodness
all around you?
Or are you blinded to it all,
shrouded in anger,
judgment, and hate?

Open your heart
to open your eyes
that you may see
from a different view.

The landscape remains the same.
It's the one seeing who changes.
If you seek the light, the beauty, and the glory
in people and places, then
that is surely what you will find.

Likewise, the dark, the negative,
the "wrong."

Take a step back
and notice
from which vantage point
you choose to experience life.

If you don't like what you see,
choose again.

Open your eyes from a place of love.
Let your heart lead you.
And, wonder at the
mystery that has eluded you
for far too long.

Your Story

The story of your life…
what do you want it to be?
What does it look like?
Feel like?
What's the message of *your* story?

Where do you choose to focus?
What perspective do you offer?

How do you want to be seen?
What do you want to represent?
How do you want to live?

Go out and write *that* story,
not the one you've bought into
or the one you've been told.

Live *your* story,
your perfect expression
of goodness and grace,
of all that you are
in Divine perfection.

This Day

The sun is up.
It's a new day,
and a new cycle of opportunity
has begun.

What will I do with this day?
How will I show up to life?
What commitments will I make?
What commitments will I keep?

Do I embrace this new day of possibility
and take my steps forward
or do I miss out
by avoiding and wasting time,
so it slips by,
unnoticed and uneventful?

Will this day matter
in the grand scheme of things?

Or is it merely
another day,
the passing of time,
the ticking of a clock,
the turning of a calendar?

The choice
is mine.

One Day at a Time

"One day at a time…"
It's more than a simple motto.
It's life.

Life happens
and life is created
one day at a time,
one moment at a time,
one choice at a time.

In every moment
and in *any* moment,
each of us is free to choose.

What will the next puzzle piece
look like?
Where will it be placed?

Will we stay on the familiar path,
the one that's worn and
comfortably laid out by us?

Or will we choose differently?
Take a tiny step
or maybe a giant leap
in a new direction?

An entire landscape
dramatically and drastically changes
with even one small move.

Yes or No?

Say "yes"
or say "no."
Which is perfect
for you right now?

Check in
and heed the call.
No right or wrong,
only what's perfect for you.
All else is noise,
outside chatter.

Your wise self knows.
Trust it.
Feel the deep inner knowing
and follow it.
Miracles will happen.

Your wise self knows
before you do.
You only have to ask.
Ask for guidance.
Ask for confirmation.

Hear the wisdom,
feel the truth,
soak it in,
and be, oh, so grateful
that this voice is always here,
always present,
eager to guide,
joyful in the
reverie of your partnership.

A Fulfilled Life

Living a life that is
fulfilling, not just full...
What does that look like?

Who do you spend time with?
What do you do?
What *don't* you do?

Where are your "yesses"
and where are your "noes?"

Who comes first?
And, who needs to go?

Paint a picture
of the ideal day –
the spaces,
the ventures,
the quiet
of your ways.

Reflection on Begin Anew

Being born is life's first big invitation. We are called to show up as the magnificent, unique beings we are here to be. As a child, we know great curiosity and wonder, and when we are able to re-enter this state, infinite possibilities lie before us.

Every moment offers us the chance to begin anew – new perspective, new choices, new beliefs lead us to new territory and possibility. Close your eyes and breathe in the possibility of "begin anew." What do you feel in your body? In your heart? Deep in your core? What is possible for you from this perspective?

A Turn into the Unknown

....

Between

Too often we live
in a land of
all or nothing,
black or white,
right or wrong.

Completely missing
the sweetness
that lies
between.

Standing on the Threshold

How often have I been here before?
In this stepping off place,
feeling the excitement that lies beyond
buzzing in my bones?

Afraid to step over.
More afraid to hold back.
When and where will I find the courage
to see...
what's on the other side?
What have I been too afraid of
or not ready to see?

Do I perch awhile longer,
leaving the mystery alone?
Do I boldly leap,
knowing I can always go back?
Or, *is* there no turning back?

It's just one step...
no big deal
(or maybe the biggest deal of all).

Without stretching a toe across,
I'll never know.

If I step across,
who will I be?
What will I leave behind?
Will I still be me?

Inner Work

Remove the veil,
lay down the mask,
and be willing to see
the truth –
the truth you were born to be.

What qualities, what gifts
do you have to offer,
are you here to share,
are you meant to give?

This is your birthright –
your destiny.

How long will you deny it,
hide it, shame it, or
apologize for it?

How hard will you make your life
by resisting what is inside you,
dying to be born?

How long will you try
to be someone else,
whisking away your own divine self
in favor of another?

You came into this world knowing,
already a full expression
of your unique, magnificent soul.

It is now your journey
to go back in –
recover and embrace
this lost spirit.
Wake it up.
Bring it out.
Love it and embrace it.

Let yourself be
all that you were born to be.

Full Expression

Do you freely and fully
express all that you are?
All that you feel?
Or do you hold it together,
shoving it neatly in a box
for fear of what will come out
if you unleash the beast?

Anger, rage, shame, frustration…
some demons that haunt.
They inhabit a dark space
deep inside,
rumbling, stirring,
craving space,
longing for expression.

How to let them out without
losing control?
What if you do "lose control,"
then what?
Is it a destructive tidal wave?
Or will letting it out be enough?

Freedom

Draw back the curtains,
lift up the blinds,
shine light onto the darkness.

Release the fear,
let go of the shame.
There is nothing to hide from here,
now that it's been given a name.

Peel back the covers,
take a look around.
The past has no hold now,
you are safe and sound.

The wounds, they were deep,
the sadness was real,
but facing it head-on
has allowed them to heal.

You are free.
Free from the grip,
free from the shame,
free to be you now,
free to release the pain.

Free to embrace beauty,
hope,
and joy.

Free to live fully
for the rest of your days.
Your courage rewarded,
your boldness expressed.
You've journeyed forever
to get here today.

The Angels Want
(Inspired by "The Materialism of Angels" by Jack Ridl)

The angels want us to belly laugh till it hurts,
exploding in silent reverie
with tears streaming down our cheeks.

The angels want us to embrace all that is –
the richness of human experience,
the fullness of life,
the depth and breadth of emotion,
longing, and yearning.

The angels want us to remember
who we are,
why we are here
and that love is our fuel.

The angels want us to dance and sing with wild abandon,
letting go of the cares of the world,
arms reaching wide,
face uplifted to the heavens,
heart open.

The angels want us to live with all our heart,
even though love always hurts,
to take the risk to glean the gold.

The angels want us to remember
what it is that makes our soul sing,
to play with our exquisite unique heart song,
to laugh, to cry, to cheer.

The angels want us to get lost in extreme ecstasy
and bathe in unimaginable grief,
allowing the emotions to wash over and through us,
cleansing, refreshing, and rebirthing as they flow.

The angels want us to *live* while we are here.

Loving Ourselves

Beating ourselves up
only wears us down.
It does not motivate us
or encourage us to change.

It begins a rapid cycle
of despair,
negativity,
and further failure.

It is only through love,
acceptance, and forgiveness
of ourselves that
we can get moving forward
again.

We need to lovingly pick ourselves up,
dust ourselves off,
as we would a loved one.

Provide comfort, care,
and understanding,
permission to be "imperfect,"
exactly as we are.

Offer loving encouragement…
we've got this,
we can do whatever
we set our minds and hearts to.

Embrace ourselves with
gentle loving support
and acceptance.

The Places We Grow

It's in the dark,
in the shadows,
where we stretch and grow.

We face ourselves
and see a new or forgotten aspect,
a piece we'd rather ignore or deny.

But there it is...
staring us down,
daring us to change,
to find a new way,
or to simply come into acceptance.

Sometimes it's about overcoming
or adjusting.
Finding a way to do this with
love, compassion,
and gentle communion.

Honoring the self...
who I am,
where I am,
what I need,
what my baggage is.

And stepping into a deeper layer,
excavating and shifting,
allowing new light in,
and new hope out.

These are the places we grow –
often watered
and nourished with tears.

Don't Lose Yourself

I see you slipping again,
slowly and silently,
into the abyss of disconnect.
The sparkle's gone from your eyes
as they look distantly through me.
I'm searching within them
for something to connect to,
past the wall of indifference
you erect as protection.
Searching...
finding nothing to land on.

Come back!
I know you're in there,
a not-too-distant memory.
Come back to yourself.
Stay lit from the inside,
your heart fire burning,
your soul awake.

Remember what it felt like
to be truly alive from within?
To feel the natural high of simply,
magnificently being you?

Come back.
Don't lose yourself to the nothingness,
the void lying between
all that you are
and all you want.
Come back.

Remember

Oh, beautiful, tortured soul,
where have you gone?
What is this beast
that consumes you,
that stole your heart?

Find your way back.
Break free from the torment
possessing your mind.
Come back from the shadows
distorting your vision,
your knowing.

Lift the veil of illusion
appearing to you as truth.

The serpent that entwines you
has choked off your breath.

Release its venomous hold,
strike down its overpowering ways.
Truth will overcome you
in the darkest of your days.

Your light is still within you,
a flicker of a flame,
yearning to grow strong again,
seeking pure expression.

Divine essence
lies buried in wait
for the demons to exit
so peace may come once more.

Find your heart,
touch your soul,
for therein lies the truth,
the love, the beauty.
Breathe from this space
to recapture your soul.

Come back, oh, dear one.
Re-enter this space in love,
in light.
Drive out the darkness
and remember.

Remember who you are.
Who you truly are.
I remember.

I beg of you...
Remember.

Reflection on Turning into the Unknown

In the twists of life that are an inevitable part of being, we often lose ourselves to confusion, doubt, fear, criticism, or stories we've told ourselves. How do we find the way back to live our lives fully and to be all we can be? When we're in the dark places that so easily drag us down and consume us, it's hard to even remember there is a way out.

Show up to Life!

....

A Prayer for Georgianna

Dear One, I wish you could see what I see:
a beautiful light in this world, unlike any other.
You shine with such radiance, openness, and grace!
You pulse with a vitality that touches lives.
Your heart is pure and divine.

Do not be afraid, Dear One.
You are whole and complete perfection.
Your light too bright to be dimmed.
Your voice too strong to be silenced.
Your vision too great to be blinded.

Step forward into this new day,
Seeing yourself as the strong, vital person you are!
A new beginning…
Limitless possibilities!
Dream BIG, Dear One!

A Soul Felt Its Worth

There is a magic that happens
the moment a soul feels its worth
and remembers
the glory it is,
the reason it exists,
the love it embodies.

The special moment perhaps
when someone mirrors back
just exactly who is there.

It shines through the eyes
of the body it inhabits
and sparkles brightly,
even in darkness.

It's a homecoming,
a reconnection to self,
to truth,
to the oneness of all.

It's a joyous reunion
of head and heart,
a merging of body and soul,
bringing life
to this human existence,
fuel for the flame
that will ignite the world.

Show Up

Show up as the light
and the Truth
you are.

Be present
Slow down
Listen

Radiate the magnificence
of your soul,
your unique being,
here to make a difference,
here to have an impact.
Here
You matter

Your presence is unlike any other.
Irreplaceable
Unique

You are the only one… the *only* one
who brings the specific
combination of gifts,
qualities, insights,
vision, and truth
that are you.

Without you showing up
ready to serve,
the world is a little more dull,
a little less radiant,
much less enlightened.

Show up and live out loud
the beauty and glory that is you!

Embracing This Life

Who am I?
Shadows,
warts,
demons and all?

What makes up
this unique blend of me?

My vision,
my rhythm,
my unique experience of life, and
my unique expression in life.

What is my purpose?
What am I here to do?
Who am I here to touch
and in what way?

What lessons are mine to learn?
The challenges, the struggles,
the opportunities...
for me,
for my growth.

This life is mine,
so let me claim it.
Let me step into it,
embracing and accepting
all of it,
even the parts I would
rather push away,
not have,
or not be...

This is me,
and I am here.
In my own way.
In my own time.

Never Doubt

My dear one,
sometimes you wonder
if life means anything
at all.

If all you do
has value, purpose,
or meaning.

Whether it makes
any difference
at all

Rest assured,
it does.

Each act of love,
kindness, and
generosity of spirit
ripples out to the world.

It may be so small
as to go unnoticed,
but the magnitude is grand.

Many small ripples
combine to become
an ocean,
a tidal wave,
a tsunami
of goodness and grace.

Never doubt, dear one.
Never.

Limitless Possibility

Your voice matters –
the chorus stronger
when you sing loud and strong.

Do not hold back
and silence
what you have to share.

Breathe in,
breathe out,
and express.

Do what you thought you never could.
Believe in yourself
and know you *are*
limitless possibility.

A Mystery

Life is a mystery.
It just is.
We waste so much time
and endless energy
trying to "figure it out."

Life is not to be analyzed,
picked apart,
or even understood.

Life is to be lived,
experienced,
felt.

Life invites us
to join in.
To be part of the party.
To sink in
and surrender
to the feelings.

Life is not tomorrow
or yesterday.
Life is not memories,
wishes, or dreams.

Life is now
Simply now
This moment
This breath
This encounter
These people
This heart
What's here right now.

Simple really…
Stop, look, listen
Feel

This is what matters
For this is what is
Breathe it in
Soak it in
Surrender
Give back to life

Life wants to dance
with you.
A willing partner
In sway and flow

Giving and receiving
Present
Transcending thought
Beyond fear
Reality is Divine

Be with what is
and breathe the breath of life
in and through your being.

Simply live
Simply love

Your Last Day

What would you do
if you learned you had
one day to live?
No second chance…
this was it.

What changes would you make?
Who would you connect with?
How would you spend your time?
What would you let go of?

Why do we act as if
we have an endless reservoir of time,
so we'll get to it "some day?"

The truth is, none of us know
when we will leave this earth.
So, why do we wait?
Why are we so out of touch
or careless with our ways
and our days?

We all know we have
limited time here.
Why do we pretend otherwise?
Why wait to forgive,
and love,
and be our full, beautiful selves?

This is so basic
so simple,
so profound,
and so overlooked.

Not wanting to
think about death,
we fail to live
as if life really mattered.

Let's wake up and begin today
to cherish the people,
the moments,
the perfect expressions of self.
And live as if today,
this moment,
was all we had.

Tragic

He died long ago,
well before
his spirit actually
lifted from his body.

Simply walking through days
a lifeless being,
merely existing,
passing time.

Dying a slow living death,
consumed by things
that don't really matter…
that drowned him alive.

Giving up all joy,
losing all energy,
present to nothing.

No heart
and barely any pulse.
Existing…barely existing.

No light from within,
all passion squeezed out
decades ago.

This is a true tragedy –
far more grievous
than the actual death.
To live, but not really.

Life is a gift, my friend.
A precious offering
to fully embrace.

Don't let this be your story.
Live today… and make it glorious!

Reflection on Show up to Life!

Once upon a time I believed I needed to control everything and was deluded enough to think I could. Once upon a time I was a perfectionist who was afraid to fail. The stories I told myself about how things "should be" clouded my reality and my ability to see a better way. They kept me in a tightly wound, serious straitjacket, always trying to "get it right" and rarely letting loose. My ability and desire to LIVE life rather than just get through it had been lost. My seriousness was in serious need of an intervention. I wanted more fun, joy, playfulness, and dreaming in my life.

For much of my life I was unforgiving of myself and deeply critical of any perceived mistake. Perfectionism led to procrastination. I avoided taking many real risks or putting myself out there. I had learned that to be liked or accepted I had to hide certain aspects of myself.

Life is calling to you and desires only for you to show up as your true self. It beckons you out of hiding, urges you to not be afraid, comforts and coaxes you to step fully in. Where can you answer these calls in a new way? What patterns and programs are you ready to leave behind? What's waiting for you when you do?

A Twist into Doubt

Slay the Dragon

Slay the dragon,
breathing fire of lies,
deceit, hatred, and
thrashing tail of bitterness,
loathing, defeat.

Stand firm, oh, brave one,
plant your feet in your truth,
touch your heart to your soul
and stand tall.

This dragon cannot harm you
when you own who you are.
Your power is mighty,
coming deep from your core.

Stare down this demon,
this monster,
to haunt you no more.

Stand tall
and breathe easy.
He is nothing at all.

Watch as he vanishes,
turning in shame,
dissolving in the shadows,
as you claim your name,
your place,
your truth,
your right.

He is gone,
and *you* are all that remains.

A Powerful Ally

Be careful the thoughts you think.
Not all of them are true.
Your mind, though a powerful ally,
can sometimes betray you.

It can lead you to the darkness
where ugliness resides
and hold you captive
with its rich, compelling lies.

All visions of the light side,
forgotten in your fear,
consumed by irrationality,
replaced with heaviness,
so strong,
it stops you in your tracks.

So, shift your mind you must
to shed those thoughts untrue.

Let them vanish,
running off of you like rain.
Bring in the thoughts of vision;
release the thoughts of shame.

Your mind is a powerful ally.
Use it wisely,
and ask it to step aside
as your heart you learn to trust.

Deep truth lies well beyond
the province of the mind,
beyond reason,
beyond logic.

When the thoughts turn murky
and eat you up inside,
close your eyes,
touch your heart,
and ask for true guidance.

Your heart and mind together
bring wisdom from your soul,
answers untarnished,
leaving lies untold.

Your mind, a powerful ally
when married to your heart,
will guide you from the darkness.

Shadows and Doubts

Shadows and doubts
cloud my sky,
blocking out my sun,
impeding my way.

I cannot see clearly
in this state,
can't get out of my own way.

All I see is gloom, fear,
uncertainty.

My racing mind
only makes it worse.
Thoughts dart and dodge in front of me,
obscuring my path,
confusing my heart.

I stand frozen,
blinded by fear,
not even remembering
how to set one foot forward.

One tiny baby step…
is all it takes
to shift this momentum,
to create a new reality.
Right now, even that feels huge
and unmanageable.

I feel drained
when I want to feel energized.
Scared where I should be excited.
Immobilized, terrified,
drowning in my own doubt.

Reflection on Doubt

We all have doubts and fears. We all have stories we tell ourselves and messages we've heard from others that keep us playing out roles that may not serve us. They may even prevent us from showing up to our fullest potential. Acknowledging these pieces within and around us will help us to move on in spite of them. Denying them or pushing them away only causes them to rise up more fiercely. So, notice them, welcome them, maybe even embrace them as you work your way through the twists of your mind and out again into your authentic self.

The closer we get to truth and purpose, the more shadows and doubt arise, begging us to play it safe, to not be so bold. What does this bring up for you in this moment?

Authenticity

....

Touch the World

Listen to the wisdom from within,
the calling of your heart,
the song of your spirit.

You know why you are here,
who you are,
and what you are meant to do.

You know you matter –
you have a special way
of touching the lives of those
around you,
of touching the world.

Let yourself out.

Let yourself express
the beauty only you
bring to the world.

Make a difference.
Soar with joy!

This is your dance,
the world is your stage...
people are waiting.

Wait no more.
The time is now.
Why do you hesitate
when the world needs you?

If You Only Knew

If you only knew
what I see when I look into your eyes,
deep into your eyes,
past the "stuff,"
down to the core.

I see a beauty beyond words.
A vast sea of possibility.
Gifts waiting to be uncovered,
waiting for you to remember.

I want to touch your soul,
to know your deepest desires,
to share your guiding dreams.

Open your heart to me,
let the light in.
I want to guide you,
to help you see
the wonder that is you.

If you only knew how beautiful you are,
how powerful you are,
how strong your presence,
how deep your thoughts,
how wise your insights,
how vast your creativity...

What would you do?
If you only knew?

Steps

Each step perfect
in its own crazy way.

The paths we walk
are ours alone
and they take us where
we need to go,
to the places we need to grow.

Through it all,
grow we will
or wither and die
in resistance, denial, refusal to see.

This life is ours –
each step brought us
to today, to this moment
with all of its gifts,
all its doubts, and
all its pain.

Where will the next step lead?

We Lose Ourselves

We lose ourselves in so many ways —
to roles,
expectations,
fears,
judgments.

We become what we think
we ought to be.

We play out roles,
pretending desperately to be
someone else —
anyone else…

We long to be like him or her,
thinking they have a magic
we surely don't possess.

What we're missing
as we lose ourselves
is this:

The most beautiful power,
the most glorious expression,
the greatest impact,
and the deepest joy
comes when we plug in fully
to who **we** are,
who we were born to be —
our unique gifts,
our divine expression,
showing up as only we can.

No envy
No limitation
No thought of "less than."

Fully expressing our magnificence,
exactly as we were born to.

Magnificent

Awaken, dear one,
and step into your life.

Stop slumbering
and sleep walking
through your days
and touch the glory
that is you.

Remember your gifts,
find your gold,
polish it up,
and let it shine
for the world!

When you awaken,
your joy is palpable,
your energy unbounded,
your impact profound.

Rise up,
come forth,
and be magnificent.
This is what you are.

Being Me

Open my eyes and ears,
clear away the cobwebs,
that I may see and hear
my truth.

Clear my voice
that I may speak my wisdom.

Open my heart
that I may love and be loved.

Rippling ever outward
a joyous expression
of what I am meant to be
and to do.

Help me to live fully,
honestly,
authentically.

True to myself
in all aspects
of my life.

Following my original instructions.
Showing up
in the glory of my existence,
embracing and embodying ME.

My light is needed in this world.
My gifts matter.
First, let me shine this light,
give these gifts,
and share my love
with myself.

For I can only give what
I have in abundance.

Vulnerability

Vulnerability...
the courage
and risk-taking
to lay yourself open
and bare your soul.

To let down the walls
a tiny bit
and let a true piece of authenticity
peek out.

To ask for something
that really matters.

To share a deep truth.
To let people experience you
beyond the mask you wear.

To open your heart,
to speak your beliefs,
to share your soul.

To be strong enough
that no matter how they respond,
it doesn't destroy you.

To be grounded enough
to be ready to really live
as you.

To throw off expectation,
judgment, or care
and wholeheartedly be
exactly who you are.

Essence

The most beautiful
expression of a being
is that which is real,
that which is true.

Emotions felt deeply and sincerely,
allowed to flow –
part of the natural course.

No restrictions
No holding back
Just pure expression

Essence shines forth
alive and illuminated
from within.
A sparkle in the eye
or the tears of heartfelt grief.

When it's genuine
and natural,
there is a simplicity
and a splendor
in whatever comes forth.

Shooting Star

Tear off the roof
and reach for the stars!
No limits!

Shoot sparkles through
your fingertips,
sprinkling love's great light
across the world.

Burst forth,
fire burning from within,
too hot and radiant
to be contained.

Expansive
Evolving
Far-reaching
Stretching through the ether,
across the Universe,
touching lives along the way
and far, far away.

Rise up
Be free
Stretch far
Touch wide

This world is yours.
Your essence
a shooting star
blasting through time and space,
leaving light, love, and truth
in its wake.

Reflection on Authenticity

It sounds simple enough to say, "Just be yourself!" I am here to tell you, there may be nothing in the world that requires more courage than to truly show up to life 100% you. It is a great risk to be willing to peel back the layers and reveal your true self. To do so is a great act of vulnerability.

Many of us grew up with the clear message, "children should be seen and not heard." If we were upset or disagreed with our parents, we were sent to our rooms. It was certainly not ok to be loud and joyful. It was not ok to express our own opinions. We were to do as we were told. Independence, carefree expression, adventure, and curiosity, were not appreciated or rewarded. So, we learned to hold back – to stifle ourselves. We learned: *It is not ok to be me.* We learned not to shine too brightly, so as not to be noticed.

I encourage each of us to shine brightly. We each have a unique purpose for being in this life and a unique expression that is only ours. No one else has our life experiences, our perspectives, our ideas, or our lessons. Therefore, each one of us is meant to touch the world as only we can and to share our gifts in our beautiful, authentic way. How might you show up just a little more true to yourself this week?

Stillness

....

True Connection

Disconnect to connect.
Break free from outside distractions,
technology, societal pulls,
mindless antics
that take us so far and
so easily away
from touching in with ourselves
and bonding with each other.

Shut out the noise,
the visual disruption,
the constant "on call."

Be present.
Be here now.
Look into the eyes of your partner,
or the heart of your own soul.
Close your eyes
to see more deeply.
Close your ears
and listen to the silence.

Find solace,
answers,
deep love
and true meaning
in the stillness,
in the white and empty spaciousness
of unfettered time.

Disconnect
to connect –
truly and deeply,
in bliss.

Presence

Wherever you are,
whatever you do,
however you feel,
be there fully and completely,
present to what is,
flowing and allowing.
Not resisting.

Life flows around us
effortlessly,
continuously,
ever-changing,
always in motion.

Be there
and allow yourself
the grace to flow,
to find the balance
between effort and ease.

Trust this is where you are meant to be,
because this is where you are.
Be certain it will
look different tomorrow,
for life is fluid,
ever-evolving,
as are we.

No two moments the same.
This is the beauty and the confusion
that is life.

In the Stillness

In the stillness
the answers come,
truths are unearthed,
promises remembered.

In the stillness
prayers are answered,
hearts are restored,
dreams fostered,
visions captured.

In the stillness
the oneness becomes clear,
connection to self deepens,
universal threads intertwine.

In the stillness
the magic lies
waiting for you to visit
and reside here,
for however many moments.

Merely Being

I am love
I am peace
I am gentleness

When I remember this,
know this,
and feel this
deep down to my soul,
my world shifts
in profound ways.

There is no need
to compete for air or space.
There is no need
to show what I know
or to prove my worth.

I merely need to be.
As a still pond
reflects the beauty around it
or a gentle breeze
grazes across the skin.

We barely notice their presence,
but the depth of their serenity
envelops us.

Reflection on Stillness

For most of my life, I didn't know the gifts that could come from slowing down and being still. I was a go-getter, determined to make things happen, and not to settle for anything less than perfect. I was raised to judge myself based on accomplishments. I didn't know how to simply *be* with myself.

Stillness and presence are precious commodities that are often in short supply in today's world. It is truly worth making time and creating space for this quality of being. This is where deep truths bubble up and the chance to commune with yourself reaps endless rewards. How can you create some stillness in your life?

A Quiet Turn

Yoga

Yoga...
Serenity,
Strength,
Balance,
Flow.

Effort...
With ease.

Going within
While reaching beyond.

Total abandon,
Freedom,
Challenge,
Victory.

A melding of body, mind, and spirit.
Home.

Sleep, Sweet Child

Sleep, sweet child,
sleep the sleep of the blessed.

Close your eyes,
drift away,
and let go of your cares...

Sink in, let go,
lay your weary body down,
and simply melt into this heavenly space.

Nowhere to go,
no need to rush,
this is your blessing.

Breathe lightly,
quiet your mind,
and delight in this precious gift.

Retreat

Time away from the routine,
from the demands,
the rush,
the distractions.

Time, simply to be,
in deep connection
with your sweet self
or with another.

Time to go within.
Time to listen to your spirit.
Time to speak with and
share the heart,
love, and
connection
that only comes from time away.

Retreat time
Getaway time
TIME
Time to let things be ok
To slip into a powerful void
of beauty, bliss, and discovery.

Floating in existence,
above the noise,
beyond the crowds,
transcending this world
to a deeper, truer space.

Peace Within

Sometimes the world feels too harsh,
too loud,
too bright.

It's time to shut down,
go within,
cuddle up,
and close out
the outside world
and noise.

Find the comfort
within your heart
in the center of stillness
that resides
deep within.

Make your way there
gently, slowly,
carefully,
reverently.

Abide here
for as long as you wish,
for as long as you need.

This is your space,
your time,
your peaceful haven
of recuperation,
rejuvenation,
renewal.

Reflection on Quiet

Sometimes when we hit a twist on our journey, the best thing to do is to do less. To *not* push through. To *not* force anything, but to allow ourselves space to rest, reconnect within, retreat from daily stresses, and find an inner peace. To seek and create a space where there is nothing to do, nothing to fix or figure out, but simply a place to slow down and rejuvenate our soul.

Closing your eyes to remove external distractions, even for a moment and connecting to your breath is a retreat and can be done anywhere. A retreat does not require vast amounts of time and money and can be as simple or as grand as you desire and are able to work into your life (as small as 5 minutes or as large as several weeks or months away). How might you apply these ideas for quiet or retreat time in the reality of your life?

Nature's Soothing Embrace

....

Let Nature Transform You

Where does your soul find peace?
Is it near the rushing of water,
the breaking of waves
calming your heart?

Is it the cool escape
of a mountainside forest?

On the beach
with sun beating down
and surf crashing on the shore?

Maybe it is in the
arctic crisp of winter air.

Most certainly there is a space
in nature.
A space where time slows down
and you are able to connect
with your own unique rhythm,
the heartbeat of your spirit.

Go there often,
either in physical reality
or in your imagination.

Close your eyes
and invite all your senses
to embody the richness
of connecting to this
precious place of yours.

Feel your internal rhythm
match that of Mother Nature
and Father Time,
as you become one
with your surroundings.

Feel your deep connection
to the entire world...
the oneness of all that is.

Soak in the magic of nature.
Breathe in the beauty of her scents.
Listen to the sounds
God created.

Feel the quality of air
as it brushes across your skin.

Look upon the ever-changing landscape
as you relish the intricacies of life.

Let nature transform you
as it claims you as its own.

On the Water

I love the water –
the rushing of the waves,
the rise and fall,
the ever-changing,
never-stopping ripples.

The gentle sound
of constant flow
washes over my heart
and brings peace to my soul.

Near the water is where I belong.
I breathe in its freshness.
I long for its cleanse.
I appreciate the tranquility
of its beauty,
its reflection of all that is.

It wraps me up
in tranquil tones
and captivates my mind.

Time stands still when I am on the water.
I feel the flow
and become one with the tide.

My rhythm of life is here.

Simple Moments

A chorus of crickets embraces me
as I gaze into the dancing flames.
Mesmerized by the glowing embers,
the colors, the constant
yet subtle movement…
pulling me in.

Under a blanket of stars
and soft cloud cover,
I close my eyes and breathe in
the bliss of this moment.

In this space nothing else matters,
time melts away,
and I am simply here.

Fully present and completely alive,
soothed by the warmth,
captivated, drawn in
to a place where all else drops away.

Peace
Heaven
Glory
In the beauty of simple moments.

Seeking Serenity

Is there a place that brings you
such peace, just by being there?
Where every breath of air softens
you gradually into a deep state
of ease and fills you with a
strong sense that
this is where I belong.

A place where the cares of the world
simply melt away and slip out of sight...
at least for awhile.

A place of relaxation, rejuvenation, even bliss...
A place where your heart sings,
your soul rejoices, and every fiber
of your being is bathed in the
incredible "rightness" of it all.

A place that sparks something inside of you
letting you know
it is part of you
and you are meant to be here.

Here you can simply BE.
Here you feel the union and
the connection with all living things.

In this heaven on earth
feel free,
feel whole.
Be serenity.

Reflection on Nature's Soothing Embrace

Connecting with nature in one way or another seems to offer a universal healing, comfort, and peace. Knowing what restores your soul and washes over you with a wave of serenity or exhilaration will guide you to your perfect nature moments. Where in nature do you feel held, safe, nourished, and nurtured? Find the place that takes you away and brings you back to your true self. Go there often.

Twisting into Turbulence

The Rat Race

Burning the candle at both ends
only fries *us* in the end.
Life's obligations
pull at us,
stretching us too thin.

Work, commitments, financial concerns
push us, drive us,
command us
to go and do at all hours,
always connected,
always available,
no request too big.
Sure, we can do more.

It is there
we lose ourselves.
We lose our ground.
We give more
than we possibly can.
We do more
than is reasonable.

Pushed by expectations
that are irrational.
Compelled by fear.
If we don't, we'll be dismissed.

Life's busy-ness consumes us,
and beats us
until we are weary
and our soul
saves us the only way it knows –
through sickness, injury, or layoff.

Anything to stop the madness
and bring some rest
unless we can find the balance,
find a way to honor the self.

There is no glory in burning out,
one more lost soul
in a wasteland of beings
striving, always striving,
to outdo one another,
to get ahead and stay ahead.

Of what?
I wonder.

Lifeline

We find ourselves lost, tossed,
and thrown into the turbulence
that can be life.

Too easily and quickly we
cast aside our lifelines –
those things that keep us
anchored, safe, and tethered
to ourselves.

We let the lifelines go
as unimportant or less important,
luxuries in an oh-so-busy life.

And we lose ourselves
to the whirlpool of insanity,
tossed and flipped and lashed
by the winds of demand.

Until we finally capsize
or run aground,
unable to weather the storm
for one more moment.

I beg you,
tether yourself
to what matters most –
love,
connection,
nourishment of body and soul,
quiet,
service,
reflection,
fun,
play!

Hold on to those who uplift you,
strengthen and fulfill you.
Release those who pull you under.
The calm is right there –
just below the storm.
It's yours for the claiming.

Inconceivable

Things happen.
We cannot imagine
or fathom
how or why.

They grip us
and tear at us
as we clench our heart
and let our tears flow.

Anguish
Sadness
Confusion
Loss

How to make sense
of the inconceivable?
Where to begin?
How to go on?

Perspective comes
in these moments
of grief.

But with little to grasp,
to anchor us
to any solid footing,
we flail, lost
and tossed
into the swirling mist
of confusion and pain.

Knowing not what we need
or how anyone can help.

Only that we are broken
(at least in this moment).

In the Dumps

When you're down
in the dumps,
it's hard to see a way out.

Everything feels like it's piling on,
falling in,
and entombing you
in the darkness of the mind.

Shadows lurk
at every turn.

Stench and distaste
spewing a giant volcano of nastiness.

No light here.
Only darkness,
and emptiness,
and lots and lots of junk.

Unwanted thoughts,
unbidden beliefs
consume and entomb.

Closing doors to hope,
optimism,
or new possibility.

We forget we know a way out.
We forget to remember
this is not forever.

The Lotus

The lotus flower –
glorious, magnificent, and radiant,
springs forth
from the mud,
untouched
and unburdened by the filth.

How does such beauty
arise out of such darkness?

Nature's reminder to us...
we need not be tarnished
by what we rise above.

And perhaps
we are more beautiful
for having risen.

Denial

"THIS CANNOT BE!"
I scream
to no one at all.
I writhe, I seethe,
my face twisted and tormented
in a hideous contortion.

Anguish
Grief
Terror
Pain

My relentless cries
into the vast emptiness
only add to the unbearable pain
of what I feel.

I clench.
I claw.
Tightening everything
beyond what I can endure.

As if...
as if that will make it stop,
change the course,
bring new hope,
rather than darken another day.

Reflection on Turbulence

It's so easy to get sucked up in the daily grind, the busyness of it all and to forget to make time for ourselves, our health, and wellbeing. It's natural to have times when we feel lost, depressed, or even in despair, not knowing how we'll ever get back to happier times.

In these moments it's important to notice, to lovingly be with yourself, and to let it be what it is – without feeling something is "wrong" or even needs to be shifted right away. Not to dwell indefinitely, but to allow the grace to be with the discomfort, to notice, to love ourselves through it, and then to choose what's next. How might you lovingly be with yourself the next time you find yourself tossing in turbulence?

Acceptance and Surrender

....

Acceptance

How often I dig my heels in
and scream to the sky,
"Nooooooo! This cannot be!"
even as it's clear
that it *is*.

Boiling with resistance
and rooted in denial,
I cling to what I
want to be true,
blind to reality,
lost in delusion,
determined to fight
with all my might.

Causing angst
and turmoil
in my beautiful mind,
tormenting my soul.

Creating unnecessary chaos
and wicked confusion,
when what is called for
is to open my eyes,
take a breath,
and begin to take in
the intricacies of life
at play,
all around me.

Shifting, moving
and happening,
whether I like them or not.

I don't have to like them
and I don't want to believe them,
even as they stare me directly
in the face,
daring me not to see.

Now is the time to lay down
the sword,
set aside the wrath,
and cease the fight
tearing me up inside.

Surrender to what is.
See where that takes me.

Finding the Flow

The secret to life
is finding the flow.

In the moments when we are stuck
and we can't see the light
or even remember there is a way out.
How do we remind ourselves
this won't last?
That it'll be ok again.

How do we take one first
tiny step forward?
And find the movement again

Through breath
Through tears
Through silence and talking it out
Relaxing, accepting, surrendering

Lay Down the Burden

Lay down the yoke.
This burden is not yours to bear.
The pain, the sorrow, the fear.
They're not yours.
And they're dragging your heart under.
It's too much to bear.

Lay down the burden, my child.
Turn it over to something more powerful than you.
Let it go
Surrender
Release…
in trust.

Your carrying it does not serve you.
Does not serve the world.
It casts a darkness
on your bright spirit.

Better that you shine your light,
find your love,
and illuminate the darkness
so others may see.

Release the frown.
Unfurrow the brow.
Get some rest.
Renew thyself.

Serenity

"God, grant me the serenity
to accept the things I cannot change,"
the familiar prayer says.

That is what I ask for today.
There is so much in my life
beyond my control.

Bring serenity, peace to my heart,
that I may allow what *is* to be,
that I may simply find a way
to be love,
to give love,
to surrender to what is.

"Surrender" – not a term of weakness,
but a state of deep acceptance,
release of my will,
and a turning over
to something mightier than myself.

Allow me the grace
to be a loving companion
on this human journey.

I pray my love
makes a difference,
my eyes reflect
to another their deeper truth,
their Divine essence,
when they can no longer see.

God, grant me the serenity
to do the hard work.

Hold Me Steady

Hold me steady
on unsteady ground.
Keep me moving forward
into the unknown.

Usher me toward my
intended successes.

Catch me when I waver,
soften the blow when I fall.

Lift me gently
and set me back on my path,
no matter the fear.

Help me to know
I am never alone.

Help me to remember
and recognize the guidance
I receive from beyond the beyond.

Walk with me
through unpredictable times.
Steer me gently back on course
and help me see the light.

Creator, I give thanks
for your companionship
on this uncertain journey.

I trust the course is clear.
I surrender to be led.
I know in my heart
I am on my way.

Reflection on Acceptance and Surrender

At times our world comes crashing in on us. Things happen that we never would have imagined, and we find ourselves lost in a sea of emotions and experiences that can consume us. It's easy to get caught up in what *should* be rather than to sink into what *is*. We can find ourselves at war with reality.

I have discovered when I give up the fight against what I do not like, I can often soften into a gentler state of acceptance. In surrender and acceptance of what is, I can breathe again, and I am no longer blind to possibility. My perception shifts and new insights may be revealed when I begin with the truth of the moment. What do acceptance and surrender look like to you?

Separate Lives

The Dance of Our Lives

Each of us
comes to this life
with unique expression,
individual gifts,
our own rhythm.

We dance through it
in our own way,
touching lives
and impacting the world
as only we can.

We are not here
to be like anyone else,
for their rhythm does not match
the beat of our soul.

It is our quest
to deeply tune in,
to connect
to what it is inside
and outside of us
making us whole and complete.

To find what brings eternal peace,
deep satisfaction,
pure contentment.
To know what makes us dance
and buzz
and feel fully alive,
as if lit from within.

This is our dance –
our spirit knows
what soothes us,
nourishes us,
and elevates us
to greater heights.

My Greatest Teachers

Thank you to my greatest teachers,
those who caused me to
look deeply at myself,
to become more than I was,
to show up to life differently.

Those who challenged me
in a heartbreaking way,
allowing me to learn life-changing lessons
through pain and discomfort.

Lessons I did not want to know,
but had to learn
so that I can remember
who I am.

Times I did not want to go through,
Feelings I did not want to have,
taught me to surrender
and let go of that
which is not mine.

I've learned to step back
and allow you your lessons
as we both journey
on our divergent paths.

I've done the best I can
and maybe missteps
aren't that at all.

Maybe each step was
just one step closer,
another nugget,
another lesson,
another gift simply disguised in ugly wrapping.

I Have Always Loved You

From the moment I knew you existed,
I have loved you in a way
I didn't understand.

When I felt you moving within me,
our bond began.
I didn't know who you were
or where you were headed,
but my love was unconditional
and eternal, even then.

I've always loved you,
even as we've grown apart,
even when my words and touch
no longer soothe your pain.

I've loved you
even when I couldn't hold you,
even when I've lost you
and you've lost me.

I've loved you in my darkest hours
when I've doubted myself
and my ability to love,
when I've had no idea how to help you.

I've loved you
as I've screamed at you,
terrified of the world
that had consumed you.

I've loved you
as I've cried out in despair,
sobbing for someone to show me the way.

I've loved you
as I have seen past the fog,
beneath the shadows
and into your heart,
your spirit,
where I have always seen and known
your wisdom, your depth, your kindness,
your love, and your promise.

I've loved you
when you cast me aside
because for me to see you was unbearable.

I've loved you
through it all.

And I will continue to love you
into eternity.

Love and Let Go, Sweet Mama

Love…
Love deeply, fiercely, completely.
And then…
Let go.

Our babies are not ours.
Know they are carried
on their own angels' wings.
Their lives are their own.
Their mission and journey, not ours.
Not ours to judge or correct.
Ours simply to love and support
and get out of their way.

So, love with all your heart,
Sweet Mama.
Then step back
and watch in wonder
as your child blossoms perfectly,
beyond your wildest imagination
into his own being,
whether it bears any resemblance
to your vision or not.

Trust, know, and allow
All is as it is meant to be.

A Parent's Love

A parent's love
runs deep,
crosses vast caverns,
stands the test of time,
flows steady,
over and through rocks,
mountains, barricades.

A parent's love
knows no bounds,
is limitless,
unending,
unconditional.

A parent's love
wishes it were strong enough,
deep enough,
grand enough
to heal all the wounds
of the child,
to mend the broken heart,
to correct the course
that seems so wrong.

And sometimes a parent's love
is strongest
when it surrenders
and lets go
of what does not belong to it.

Remaining true,
constant, and ever-present,
but unable to do more.

Untethered

Lost in another's troubles,
someone you hold so dear
and love so deeply,
someone you cannot save
no matter how your heart breaks.

There isn't enough pain
you can feel
to make another life better.

Feeling the pain
rips into your joy,
shatters your productivity,
makes life feel like a sham.

What else matters?
What else could matter?

If this is so bad,
so off-track.
If you can't help this one,
how can you help anyone?

How can you have joy,
feel success?
Can you?
Or is it all a big façade,
a mask you wear to soldier on?

Utterly powerless in one space,
yet mighty overall.
Your life is separate,
as is your mission.
Your joy not tethered to another.

Fight your way out of this
cavernous emptiness.
Back to wholeness.

Reflection on Separate Lives

It is easy to get caught up in the pain of another, especially someone you love deeply and dearly... especially if that someone is your child. Finding a way to let go so each of you can find your own way is perhaps the hardest choice in life.

Discovering we can have joy and create a life, even when someone we love is suffering and struggling is a gift and a challenge. We can only walk our path, sending love and compassion to those in our world as they find their way. Finding a way to love and let go all at once... herein lies the opportunity.

Finding Grace

Message from Above

You are never alone,
Dear Child.
You forget this
and forget all you have to do
is call, ask, speak, think, listen,
and I am here by your side,
in your heart.

Open your heart to me,
close out the noise.
Slow down,
hush now,
and tune in.

You will feel my steady presence,
my willingness to go where you lead,
my love,
my undying support.

I hold you gently, tenderly,
in a space of love,
a cloud of acceptance,
a breath of faith.

Believe
Remember
Reach out
Especially when you forget.

Grateful

Thank you, God,
for hearing me
above the din,
amidst the noise.

Thank you for getting through to me
when I make the time for you.

Creator, Great Spirit, Universe,
whatever you may be.
All I know is there's a power
much greater than me.

What a relief that is.
I don't have to do this alone.
If I only take the time
to quiet myself,
silence the outer distractions,
sink into nature,
or simply close my eyes,
and breathe.

What a blessing to be guided,
to trust and allow,
to find the space to be here now.

It fills me with serenity
to find this place of calm.
Thank you, Great Spirit,
for holding me in your loving grace.

Best We Can

We do the best we can
with what we have,
with what we know,
with what we feel.

It's all we can do,
and it's enough.

Expect no more.
Let it be enough.
Let yourself sleep at night,
not wondering
if you could have done more.

Let the peace be there,
feel it to be true.

The restless wondering
does not serve.

Each moment –
simply check in,
do the best you can
and then let it go.

Center

How to find the ease
within a deeply challenging place?

Through breath,
presence,
release,
surrender,
acceptance.

Allow grace to enter in
where effort used to be.

Find flow,
balance,
and ground.

Be real with what is
Allow the experience
Allow the emotions
Then find your center,
and carry on.

Guide Me Gently to Grace

Let the breeze blow away
my cares and concerns,
soften the worry lines on my face,
release the heaviness
that burdens me.

Take away the challenge
that is not mine
to bear.

Wash away the sadness,
remove the grief.

Let me drift into
a hollow of peace.

Lift up my heart
so I may breathe.
Guide me gently to grace.

Grace

Allow grace in.
Let it light its way
gently into your existence.

Grace, the beautiful state
of ease and flow.

In grace there is an ethereal quality,
a Divine guidance,
a trusting, knowing,
and allowing.

A delicate touch of grace
allows things to be ok
exactly as they are.

Grace invites you
merely to show up,
be present,
and go with life.

No force
No resistance
Just floating forward
in the beauty of
what is,
enveloped and swaddled
in Divine perfection.

Reflection on Finding Grace

At times my shadows still reappear. These pieces live within me and it is only now I am learning to be tender with them – to know them and lovingly embrace them as part of who I am.

When I get out of the way, grace comes forth more easily. When I step aside, take a breath, and allow myself to trust and be led, life flows more smoothly. Grace is the ultimate state of surrender somehow exuding and assuring me things will be all right. Grace reminds me that I am not alone on this life journey.

Lost in Confusion

Wondering

Can't breathe...
walls caving in,
pressure mounting,
doubt surrounding
and engulfing me.

Can I handle this?
Do I have what it takes?
Where will I find the strength,
courage,
energy
to push on and push through?

Where can I find support?
Who are my allies?
Who's on my side?

Who truly wants my success?
Who's invested in me?

How do I remember
to connect
to the deeper source
within and beyond me
that can get me through anything?

That always wants me to succeed?
That answers my every call...
if only I remember to ask.

The source of energy, courage,
and strength beyond
whatever I have on my own.

When I plug in there
my own smallness
no longer matters
because I am a part of
a magnificent Universe –
my greatest supporter.

Powerless

When I find myself powerless,
my heart and mind
churning endlessly,
desperately seeking a foothold,
grasping for an idea,
a clue as to anything
I can do
to make a difference.

Coming up empty,
time and again.
Gasping for air.
Screaming into the Universe.
Crying out to no reply.
Desperation streaming from my pores.

Spinning and whirling
into deeper confusion,
mind-numbing grief.

Where is the silver lining?
Is this a blessing in disguise?
I scoff at these
simple platitudes
falling, meaningless,
into the pit of my reality.

"Have faith," my friends say.
"No!" (or something worse)
I want to scream back.

There is no simple salve
to soothe a wound so deep,
no shiny vision
to lead me on.

Not in this moment
of darkness and loss.

There will be,
some part of me knows.
But not right now.

Confusion

Swirling in the mist of doubt,
lost,
confused,
questioning.

Newness all around me
Unfamiliar
Rocky, shaky ground
Where do I go from here?

There are veils and shadows
sneaking all around.
No clear direction,
only a fog turns me around.

My heart pounds,
head spins,
mind races,
as answers elude me.

In this state I can find no hope
of clarity or certainty
or even of how or where to begin.

Need to stop,
take a breath,
close my eyes,
re-ground, re-set,
and go within.

Listen
Shut out all the noise
My answers lie within me
They will not steer me wrong

Don't Let Me Lose Myself

Don't let me lose myself
to the madness that surrounds you.

Let me stay grounded
in the truth of me.

Connected to my wise self,
remembering all I know and
all I've learned.

Let me create my own time and space.
Allow me room to breathe.

Let me stand my ground
and anchor in **me**,
claiming my space,
standing tall,
standing firm.

So whatever winds of turmoil
rage around me,
it is in myself where I find comfort,
peace, ease, solace…
where the familiar still resides.

My ground does not need to be blown away
by the chaos of outer worlds.

My peace, my calm
lie within me.

Let me remember
to connect within
when times get tough.
Don't let me lose myself.

Clouds

What's happened?
The skies were blue, the roads were clear…
And suddenly, it's darkening.
Down to one lane, slowing,
darkness closing in.

Where did the road go?
Lost in a cloud,
no guideposts beyond a faint blinking light ahead.
Blindly inching forward,
trusting somehow
we will get through,
we'll be ok,
that onward is the only choice.

But we can't see…
One false move will throw us into the ditch,
too fast and our traction will fail,
too slow and we may get stuck,
unable to move.

So we clench and we shake
and we try to breathe
as we slowly inch forward.

How long will it last?
It's heavier now,
coming faster than we can keep up with,
unable to clear,
unable to breathe,
unable to see.

Where are we?
How much further?
Can we endure?
Slipping, sliding,
gripping, grinding,
hoping, praying,
knowing somehow this can't be the end.
Boldly onward.
No way to turn back.

Then, suddenly, out of nowhere…
is there a peek of brightness?
Yes, there's hope!

We can see a little further now,
go a little more quickly,
gain a little more traction,
breathe,
slow the heart,
ungrip the wheel.

A light out of this cave – it really is.
And, then, as abruptly as it came on,
the darkness is lifted
and we're back in the sun.
Smooth sailing…
until the next cloud.

That stretch behind us,
a brief moment in a much longer journey,
so very powerful
in its terrifying grip.
Its memory still shakes us
long after we're clear.

But, it's bright now, sunny and bright.
We can release now
and for the moment, sail again in joy,
in ease, in peace.

Stronger than You Think

You're stronger than you think,
mightier by far
than anything life can
hurl your way.

Your strength emanates from
a deep, deep core,
an endless reservoir of love and light
that fuels you.

Even when you feel you can't go on
and you can't see the light,
this strength pours to you
and through you,
urging you to merely lift your head,
to take one more breath,
to move one more step.

And, slowly, bit by bit,
the strength grows stronger.
It will not fail you now.

You're so much stronger than you think,
my dear.

Reflection on Lost in Confusion

As quickly as we may experience a moment of grace, the winds may shift and once again we find ourselves upset and unsettled.... this is the rhythm of life. We may hide out for a while or we may coast numbly onward, one leaden step after another. We may doubt everything we knew not so very long ago as the current shadows engulf us. We may forget how to connect to our sources of strength and inspiration, feeling neither. The invitation is to remember this is a temporary shift.

Inner Guidance

....

Silence

We fear it,
even as we long for it…
wondering what we will discover
in the uncluttered moments,
alone with ourselves.

Our mind fights mightily,
fearing it might be forgotten
or dismissed.

Yet it is in this space of stillness
where beauty, wisdom, insight, and inspiration
creep out of the shadows,
finding their way beyond cobwebs of thought.

No doing or force,
pretending or trying.
Simply being.
In the silence.

Truth is revealed and ideas are born
when we dare to shut out
the great cacophony of outside voices, opinions, ideas,
and believe we hold within ourselves
all we need.

In the space of not knowing
we remember and discover
who we are, that we are enough,
that we know enough to begin.
Right here.

Life springs forth from silence
and leads us where it may…

Choices

Each day, each moment,
choices are made.
Choose wisely, Dear One.

What matters the most?
What brings you great joy?
What fills up your soul?
And brings you to life?

Choose wisely, Dear One.
The distractions are many,
clear guidance lacking.
Listen to your heart.
Listen deeply,
listen true.

Do not be distracted
Do not be confused
Your soul knows your answer
Breathe in,
listen,
then choose.

A Walk with Essence

Walk hand-in-hand
with your essence
and step onto a
magical path,
connected and enveloped in
deep truth,
solid knowing,
and profound guidance.

This journey will take you far.
Each step intended, created,
for your highest good.
A step along your life path.
Not knowing where it will lead
or how far it goes,
but stepping on with love,
joy, and trust.

Accompanied by the
strongest partner you have.
Embrace and be embraced
by all that you are.
Breathe it in.
Sink into this place
of true connection to self,
and reside here often.

In this space, you cannot go wrong.

Answers Lie Within

Journey within
to find your truths,
to find your answers,
to access your inner compass,
your wise guidance.

You are more than you
have ever been told.

You are greater than
you could ever imagine.

And your answers
do not come from others,
not from books,
not from courses,
not from studying
your whole life long.

Your answers lie within.
Find them,
touch them,
embrace them,
and live them.

Finest Expression

Find your own way.
Chart your course.
This life is yours,
and yours alone.

Huddle up with yourself
and your highest team.
Call in your angels and guides.
Know you are never alone.

Be very present
to the wisdom emerging
in the stillness,
in the silence,
in the bliss
where outside voices
are silenced.

What feels right to you?
What touches your soul?
Excites your heart?
Calms your nerves?

What feels a little bit scary
and a lot exciting?

Pay attention
Go there
Test it out

This is the wisdom
that calls you forth
into your finest expression
of self, truth, purpose.

Within You

Walk through life
knowing all you need
to create peace, love, joy,
balance, and connection
is within you.

When you are tuned in
to your higher self,
your inner wisdom,
the wise one who knows your rhythm,
your needs, your nourishment,
and you listen and respond to
the guidance you receive,
you will flow more easily through your days.

You will find grace in expression.
You will feel acceptance
of self and others.

There will be a spaciousness
and an expansiveness
around you,
inviting your limitless potential
into being,
coaxing it ever onward,
drawing it out,
and releasing it.

Everything you desire
must first emanate
from you.

Listen

Listen —
really listen…
deeply listen…

What do I know
but choose not to hear?

What do I hear
but choose to ignore?

Listen to myself —
my best answers are within me.

Listen to others —
what wisdom do they offer?
What can I learn by listening
to their insights and experience? their fears?

Listen to my judgment of others —
what does it tell me about *me*?

Listen…
really listen…
stop talking,
stop thinking,
stop analyzing,
stop showing off,
and just listen!

For one day,
one hour,
one moment…
What will I hear if I really listen?
What will I learn?
Where will it take me?

Reflection on Inner Guidance

For most of my life I've been content to play it small, to hide out and to go unnoticed. I didn't want to ruffle any feathers or make any waves. I was content to rely on the wisdom of others for everything, even things as important as raising my family. I had no idea I had a far superior inner guidance waiting to be heard. I certainly didn't trust myself.

The truth is when I find myself really squirming in discomfort over confusion, fear, sadness, or grief, my immediate temptation is to turn outside of myself for guidance, support, encouragement, reassurance. While there is nothing wrong with having support systems in place, this takes me away from *feeling* what's going on for me. It takes me away from being with myself first, and trusting my inner wisdom to know what's right for me in this moment. No matter how well intentioned others are, they don't know my heart and spirit or what I truly need. Without comforting and loving myself first, I don't learn to trust the one who always walks with me. I miss a chance to reinforce the idea that I will not abandon myself.

Nothing is more important than taking time for stillness, reflection, and connection with my heart and spirit when it comes to keeping my life on course or getting back on track when I've been thrown into the weeds. Rather than desperately searching outside of myself for someone to tell me what to do, I need to remember my truest answers come from within. I can't access them if I'm surrounded by chaos or listening to too many other voices. Stillness and reflection are core practices to providing strength, wisdom, and inspiration.

Be Real

....

Lean In

Lean into your being,
lean into your soul,
lean into your feelings,
embrace them all.

The ugly,
the scary,
the dark,
the fear,
the shadows,
the gremlins.

They're real
and they're there.

Avoiding does nothing
to make them go away.
Stuffing and denying
only sets them free
to eat you alive from the inside,
their fire growing stronger,
fueled by your denial.

So, lean in,
feel them,
be with them,
giving them space,
and honoring them
as part of your whole.

Welcome them
to release them.

Let Me Be

Let me be
where I am.

Held hostage
by the story
my heart clings to right now.

Your discomfort with *my* pain
is not reason enough
for me to release it.

Just stand by me,
give me your love,
lend me your strength,
and offer your prayers.

Don't make me explain
or defend
a pain I hope you never know.

Don't try to wash it away
or brush it off.
This is real
and this is deep.

It's mine
and this is where
I need to abide
for awhile.

Just allow me
the grace to be
exactly where I am.

Challenging Passages

There are times in life
when a smooth sail
suddenly goes bad,
and we find ourselves
tossed and turned
in unknown, uncharted
turbulence.

The sun vanishes
and darkness looms,
swooping in as if out of nowhere.

We hunker down
and ride it out
for we missed our chance
to escape to safety.

No choice but to
sail on through –
over and through the chop of the wake,
wind rushing,
lightning crashing.

Scary for the time being,
yet finite in its power.
This too shall pass.

Reflection on Being Real

For as long as I can remember I have tried to push away the uncomfortable feelings: anger, fear, shame, unworthiness. I have learned to hide the "ugly" parts of myself, while hating them and wishing they would just go away. I have denied aspects of me that didn't make me proud and shut down parts that weren't liked or accepted by others.

We all learn through the years what others are comfortable with, who they want us to be, how they want us to show up, so we conform… possibly crushing ourselves along the way.

I'm learning to lean into whatever I'm feeling, to be with what's here, and to embrace all aspects of me. I invite you to play with these ideas as well. For it is in the being, welcoming, and leaning in, we can find spaciousness, peace, and free ourselves from things we have denied in the past.

Shared Journeys

Wish I Could Do More

There's little I can do,
and that's hard for me.
I feel your pain
and I want to wash it away,
leaving you fresh and whole,
unblemished,
as if it were never there.

But, of course, it's not possible,
and it's not for me to do.

Better I hold space,
send love,
reach out,
be your loving support
and safe place to land,
should you choose.

Please know how deeply
I love you, my sweet,
how much I wish you peace,
and that I send healing waves
your way.

I hope it matters
and somehow you feel me there
in your darkest hours,
and the love
crossing the distance
finds your heart
and soothes your soul,
if only for a moment.

The Web of Your Life

Weave a web,
an intricate, expansive
web of support,
encouragement,
and connection.

The people who are here
to journey with you,
to walk side by side,
or alternately leading
and then following.

Those who inspire you
and are inspired by you,
who share in your victories,
and champion your work,
who share their lives
and their visions,
who let you lift them up.

In this exquisite web
magic happens,
abundance flows,
dreams are fulfilled,
and burdens lessened.

Right people, right time.
No doubt.
Trust and allow as you
organically spin
this web of your life.

Hearts Intertwined

Good friends,
sad times,
distinct and similar paths.

My heart breaks
as your tears fall.

Together we buoy
each other up
for the next volley
life serves our way.

Together is better –
there's strength there.
Somehow we find laughter.
We share light,
and we offer hope.

Shared love
through fear and sorrow
builds us up
to keep on
keeping on.

Good friends,
shared times.
Love.
Hearts intertwined.

Come with Me

Come with me
as we soar
to heights unknown.

I want you with me,
beside me
always.

Together
as we journey on.

Sailing on a
magic carpet ride
to distant lands
as fantasies come to life.

Come with me.
Share the joy,
the amazement,
the fascination
of new doors opening,
new possibilities revealed,
and new realities shine forth!

Come with me
and stand by my side,
my partner for life,
my rock and my guide.

Be the One

Be the one
who looks through
the eyes of love.

Beholding all you see
in reverence
of their divinity.

Seeking the beauty within,
looking below the surface,
connecting to the true self
buried deep within.

Follow the eyes
deep to the heart of the soul.

Find what is pure
and good
and blessed
in the people you meet.

See their humanity
and find your connection.
What bonds you together,
not what tears you apart.

We are one –
one energy,
interconnected
in all ways.

A Showering of Grace
Dedicated to my dear, sweet Mama

Six dimes fell down from heaven
this morn
to remind me of her face,
her gentleness,
her innocence,
her kindness,
and her grace.

She lived life fully,
appreciating the simple things –
a sweet dessert,
a tender touch,
a shared smile.

She always gave the benefit of doubt
to those whose paths she crossed.

Today this will remind me
to leave the world better
than I found it.

To bring my own gentleness
and love.

To make a difference
through kindness.

Thank you,
Beauty from above.

Reflection on Shared Journeys

Our lives are better when we share them with those who offer deep love, acceptance, and connection, who know how to be there for us and allow us to be there for them. To have loved ones, friends, and mentors who really want you to shine and who let you in to help them shine – this is a gift. And, so I invite you to create a web of people who fill you up, nourish your spirit, and challenge and inspire you to be your greatest. Who might be in your web?

Rebirth

Healing

I feel the peace
sink in
like a balm
upon my soul.

Healing is here.
Healing is happening.
My heart is reawakening.
Love replaces pain.

Memories of past hurt
flicker in the distance,
nothing more than a glimmer
replaced by a deeper truth
of always-present serenity.

A new day is upon us.
A new chapter unfolding –
one day at a time,
one moment, one instant
at a time,
adding up to Divine perfection,
returning me to myself.
Returning me to love.

Truth

Gaze softly upon yourself
through eyes of love.
Look deeply into the soul,
and see yourself as your
Creator does,
as the Universe gazes upon you.

In this space
there is only beauty,
only perfection,
even when clouded
by shadows and fear.

But look deeply, my child.
The truth lies deep
beneath the surface
no matter how many
masks you wear
nor how many layers
you've donned.

A light lies within,
unafraid to shine,
waiting to be recovered,
yearning to be brought forth
into this world –
longing to share its beauty with
all it touches.

Nurturing New Life

It is up to us
to create fertile soil,
a birthplace within,
for beauty to spring forth.

We must nourish this space
with love.
For bitterness spoils this ground
and lays to waste
whatever might have been.

It is through love and light,
joy and forgiveness,
that radiance flourishes.
Not in the darkness of
resentment and despair.

Vitality, strength, resilience
spring from a pool of hope,
faith, and
belief in a greater vision.

Dreams bring light.
Faith strengthens root.
Hope draws forth the tender sprouts
of new life.

Heal Thyself

Heal thyself, Dear Child.
For this is where it must begin.
Nothing outside of you
can take away your pain
or soothe your soul.

Healing is an inside job
and you have all you need
in your heart,
in your precious, gigantic heart,
and in your glorious soul.

Your light and love
will soothe your soul,
calm your pain,
and release all dis-ease.

Bring in ease.
Let in light.
You are perfect, whole,
healthy, and complete.

Embrace this as
your birthright
and move forward in
a state of grace,
wholly renewed,
into your new life.

Free Yourself

Can you imagine…
what it would be like
to live with abandon,
throwing caution to the wind,
and embracing life exactly as it is?

Laughing out loud without care,
singing and dancing like no one is watching.

Fully, totally, and completely
expressing the very core of your being.
Feeling your feelings…
all of them.
Embracing them, welcoming them,
and allowing them their course.

Living in a space of respect, honor, and awe.
Amazing and surprising yourself.
Swirling and twirling carelessly,
taking your steps with trust,
following the lead of an unseen force.

Noticing, wondering, and appreciating
the glory and magnificence that is you.

Throw off the shackles that bind you,
limit you,
and free yourself
to this glorious life
that is yours for the claiming.

This Pure, Precious Moment

Wherever you are,
take it in.
The beauty and glory
of this space.
The colors,
sounds,
feelings.

Find the wonder
and cherish it now.
For this is the present.

Breathe it into your soul,
feel your heart swell.
Close your eyes
to feel fully
the exquisiteness
of this moment.

This pure, precious moment
is a gift in itself.
A beginning, a middle, an end.
A pause
in the symphony of life.

Cherish it
and honor it
as Divine perfection.

Maybe these are reminders
of times gone past,
of people, places, and things
that have touched your heart,
touched your life.

Maybe there is a promise
of tomorrow.
But past and future
are merely illusions in this space.

This beautiful space of now,
of all that is.
It beckons to you,
inviting you to notice,
to be present,
and to join in
this dance.

For in this moment
your future is born
and your past renewed.

Rise Up!

Rise up, oh Phoenix!
Blazing firebird
across the sky.
Leaving a trail of luminescence
in your wake,
illuminating a path
for those who will follow.

Rise up and shine on.
Yours is not a destiny
of darkness.
Your light must carry on.

Born again, born anew...
a new day is dawning
and so are you.

Rise up
Rise up and soar
Let no man hold you down.
Let nothing clip your wings.

Blaze your glory
Leave your mark

Reflection on Rebirth

For so very many years, I didn't know there was a way to make myself a priority and still be a good mother, daughter, wife, or friend. It felt selfish or wrong.

When I did follow my passions and make time for following my dreams, I was cautioned I "better take care of my husband" (so he didn't leave me). I was often asked by friends, "Who's watching your kids?" and was told how lucky I was because it was my husband (who also happens to be their father). Messages were everywhere telling me this scenario really wasn't ok and I was incredibly fortunate. I should probably even apologize for my wonderful life.

Each day offers a new beginning, a chance for healing, for forgiveness, and for possibility. How we interact with life and its moments determine whether we find hope, serenity, and openness or stay stuck in pain and unhappiness. Healing is always there – just waiting for you to tap into it, to open your heart and receive universal love.

Gratitude

Old Me, New Me

Old Me watches in amazement
and chuckles at New Me's ways –
open,
expressive,
out there!

Of course, New Me is really
Old Me long forgotten...
an exuberant child
full of joy,
bursting with curiosity,
and ceaseless energy!

Coming to life again
with the spark of remembrance
of who "Me" really is.

Old Me stands witness
to New Me finding her way
back to the light,
the love,
the joy,
the pure beautiful, exquisite
expression of self!
And both Me's celebrate
this long-awaited reunion.

Illumination

Light shines brightly from within
Inside out to the world
Casting away shadows
Searing through doubt,
Sprinkling divine essence all about

Coming alive from within,
Uncontainable joy,
Excitement and wonder,
Reverence and awe,
Alignment with purpose,
Undeniable truth.

A call from within
to step forth,
to go through,
in spite of the darkness,
no matter the fear.

This light won't be buried
or hidden no more.
It's here!
A heart light
touching lives, near and far,
answering the call
to be *all* you are meant to be.

I Am Blessed

I am blessed to be blessed.
To have vision that sees possibility.
To rarely focus on lack.
To have a burning inner determination
to make things happen
and also a surrender
allowing things to flow.

I am blessed with a love for learning
and a hunger for growth
fueling my constant evolution.

I am blessed with curiosity and wonder
that leave me wanting more.

I am blessed with a heart and a spirit
that speak to me in ways
that I cannot ignore.

I am blessed to see opportunity
everywhere.

I am blessed to see beauty
and to feel and create joy.

I am blessed to pull myself up and out
when times get hard
and it feels dark and scary.

I am blessed with many teachers
who show up
at just the right time.

I am blessed with love and connection.
I am blessed with authenticity
and a desire to simply be me.

I am blessed with a mindset and a spirit
that have always known
there's always a way.

I am blessed to savor my blessings.

A Prayer of Gratitude

Creator, I give thanks
for the many, many blessings
in my life.
For life's sweetness
and life's sorrows.
For lessons learned,
and lessons still to come.
For the limitless opportunities
that are there
when I open my eyes
and heart to notice.

I give thanks
for love and for loss.
For a life richly lived.

Thank you for watching over me
and for standing by my side.
For being there
even when I am blind
and especially when I am lost.

Thank you for always
helping me find my way back.
Back to my path
and back to my way.

I am grateful
for life itself.
For the beauty all around me,
for the beauty within me,
for being able to see
the beauty in each one of us.

Thank you for sunrise and sunset,
for full moons
on darkest nights.
For fireflies who dance,
and hawks who soar,
reminding me of
beauty, grace, and vision.

Thank you
for all I have,
all I am,
and all I may give
to my world.

Thank you.
I am eternally blessed.

Reflection on Gratitude

Gratitude is one of the most powerful practices I have embraced. Every single day presents things I am grateful for, no matter how bad a day may look or feel. By tapping into gratitude, I send myself into my next hours able to soak in the beauty of my life with true appreciation. My state of mind shifts when I can find gratitude I couldn't imagine seeing, and this opens me up to more things to be grateful for. I invite you to make gratitude a regular daily practice and notice how your life changes!

Closing

Circling back to where we began, let me say again, my shadows and old programming remain even as I grow and evolve, stretch, and learn. Gremlins still challenge me, and I have to work to keep myself moving forward. What I have learned throughout my life is powerful, and unlearning old ways is no easy feat. I believed putting myself first was selfish and thinking about myself was egotistical – in other words, very, very wrong.

For the past decade or so, I have discovered a healthier way – a way to honor my being, to express my spirit, and to bring my unique self to life. When I am true to myself, I am better in every arena and for everyone else because I am coming from a well-nourished, well-loved foundation. If I don't love and honor myself, I will always be seeking someone else to fill these voids within me – something no one else can do. I will never truly be able to love and honor another if my own needs have not been met. When I honor myself and let my light shine with no holding back, I show up to the life I was born to live.

I am living my life full out and I'm here to invite and encourage you to do the same – claim your life (*all of it*), step into your potential, see your greatness, and let it out so the world is illuminated brightly by souls following their hearts and fulfilling their destinies.

I didn't know it was ok to be imperfectly me. I thought I had to be a perfect mom, raising a perfect family, which meant being in control and holding it all together. I now know there is only so much I can control – namely, me. Even my kids have their own life paths and plans. Sometimes the best thing I can do is give my love and support, and then let go of that which is not mine.

I tend to over rely on my mind and "figuring things out." Only in the past few years have I moved from head to heart for wisdom and guidance – to trust, rather than to know. I've learned curiosity may be more powerful than knowing, so I try to look at life through the eyes of wonder – curious, inquisitive, and open.

I am willing to step back and witness myself going through life, and I invite you to do the same. Be ready and willing to be surprised, for when we give up having to figure it out, we may well be amazed at what comes our way!

Let go of what you think you know and how you think things "should" be to settle into your current reality. Trust what is coming may be better than you've ever dreamt.

Let go of believing you know what's right for anyone, *even yourself.* Surrender to the next step of your journey. Step confidently on to your labyrinth of life. Don't hold back. Take risks and ask for what you need and want. Allow yourself to receive support. Trust and be present. Sink in and embrace this human existence. And, journey on, one step at a time… that's all that is ever asked of you.

Walk the Labyrinth

Enter with a question
and begin the long and winding journey.
One footfall at a time,
letting go of the need to rush,
noticing the feelings that may come
at an unexpected turn –
a turn that takes you away
from the prize you so anxiously seek.

This step
Here
Now
This very next step
It's all that matters

Find your own rhythm,
find your own pace,
and surrender to being led –
into the unknown
and out again.

In the space of slowly moving forward
can you simply be with yourself,
allowing the answers to come?
Hearing the wisdom flowing
as you journey on.

Can you trust your foot will fall on the path
and if it bumps up against the rock wall, it's ok?
Knowing you'll be guided back
to your path.

Can you soften your gaze
and maybe even look up
and take in the beauty all around?
As you move forward
steadily, slowly,
in your own time.

Noticing, appreciating the beauty
and the wonder in each moment.

This is life...
each step marks a moment.
A moment forward to the end,
sometimes moving too slowly,
sometimes too quickly...
and we miss out in impatience or hurry.
Sometimes settling into the being-ness of now.

There is no end point to arrive at –
it's all just part of the journey.

Raise your eyes to the heavens,
take in the magnificence and richness
all around,
and surrender to the footfall,
trusting...
you *will* be led.

Acknowledgements

Where do I begin to acknowledge and express my deep gratitude for the many people who have walked this path with me and helped me be where I am today? I am truly honored and blessed by the people who have showed up in my life to offer their support and encouragement. I am grateful to all of the people in my life who have supported me, challenged me, and presented me with many opportunities to experience the richness of life. It is humbling, to say the least.

To my friends who have been there for me through the dark and the light, cheering me on and lifting me up each step of the way, reminding me I am not alone and I don't have to figure everything out by myself, I am eternally grateful. For those who have held the vision of this book over the past two years: Deborah Bussewitz, my friend and retreat partner, you were there at the very beginning and have been here every step of the way, walking with me through so much; thank you for reading, editing, and coaching me through the creation of *111 Invitations*. Steve Aman and Jen Dietrich, my Mastermind partners who never lost faith in what I could create and have helped me to believe it myself, you saw great things in me even when my own light felt so very dim, and together we have created what I could not have done alone. Kristin Conway, my WGSS, you are in my heart and on my path walking side by side with me through all of life, and I am unbelievably grateful. Ellen Fabrowicz, my long-time friend and sister, thank you for reviewing my earlier drafts and offering your insight, wisdom, and encouragement; thank you for seeing things in me I often overlook and holding a higher vision of what I can achieve. Allyn Stelljes, thank you for reading, iting, and offering your energy, love, and purple hearts to my ork! Amy White, thank you for your endless support, for reading nd deeply understanding what my book is about and capturing it n the foreword. Karen Theresa Waldron, thank you for listening so often… to my life experiences, to my fears and doubts, and to these words, and for being one of my greatest champions along the way, offering your undying support and wisdom. Mary Lally, thank you for being the one I can always call on to bring humor, laughter, love, wisdom, and lightness into my life!

To those on the Australia Hay House 2012 cruise with me who have carried energy for this book to be born: Leanne Price, Sheila Schuster, Leon Beaton, thank you! What a joy to share this journey with you. To my writing friends from Taos, thank you for helping me stretch and become a better writer. Thank you for witnessing and supporting me. I am especially grateful to my Story Stewpot Sisters, Mary, Judy, Yoli, and Fredi, for holding space for exploration, vulnerability, and creation. To Heaven McArthur, thank you for the gorgeous cover image and thanks to Mindy Meiering, whose beautiful image and energy grace this cover.

To my teachers who have supported me and helped me to believe in myself and step into the world in a new way: Ross Quinn, thank you for seeing me, believing in me, and pushing me to be all that I could be before I could see myself. Laura Berman Fortgang, thank you for inspiring me to be who I want to be in all my ventures, no matter what I do! Renee Trudeau, thank you for providing the safe, supportive, and accepting space which opened me up to connection with my Wise Self, for teaching me not to abandon myself, and for encouraging me to show up to life 100%. Jen Louden, thank you for letting me know that I matter, for showing me how to embrace all of life and all of myself, for believing in me as a writer, and for intuitively helping me find the beautiful labyrinth structure of this book. HeatherAsh Amara, thank you for helping me to tap my warrior goddess energy so that I can both push through and receive! Julia Cameron, it was in your workshop two years ago, on the weekend of my 50th birthday that this book was conceived and evolved. I am also grateful to the magical energy of Kripalu Center for Yoga & Health, where I met some of these teachers, where the book was born, where the title emerged, and where I am transformed each time I visit.

Thank you to those who read my drafts and offered input: Allyn, Amy, Ellen, Tom, Mary, and Deb – I couldn't have gotten to this finished product without your help and for that I am eternally grateful. To those who offered to read and share testimonials: Jen Louden, Renee Trudeau, HeatherAsh Amara, and Laura Berman Fortgang, I am so honored to have your support and deeply appreciate your time and feedback. Thank you to my production team at Balboa Press and my editor, Annalisa Parent, for turning my dream into a beautiful reality.

And, finally to my family: Tom, thank you for your loving support, encouragement, grounding, and belief in my dreams as well as your editing insights. Thank you, honey, for your love, your undying support and constant partnership through this project and all of life. Thank you for your willingness to hold down the fort during my time away at the retreats and workshops that have nurtured me and brought this book into being. And, to my boys, Nate and Adam, thank you for showing me how to love unconditionally and for inspiring me to be my best. I love you all and would not be where I am or who I am without you in my life.